Mathematics Assessmen
Concepts and Terms in Large-Scale Assessment

Lew Romagnano

The Metropolitan State College of Denver
Denver, Colorado

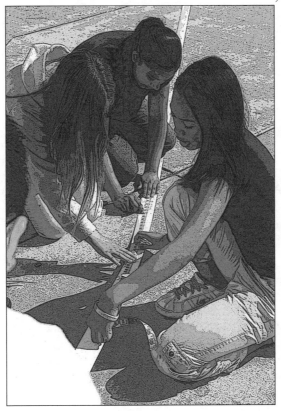

NCTM ® | NATIONAL COUNCIL OF
TEACHERS OF MATHEMATICS

Library of Congress Cataloging-in-Publication Data

Romagnano, Lew.
    Mathematics assessment literacy: concepts and terms in large-scale
assessment/Lew Romagnano.
        p. cm.
    Includes bibliographical references and index.
    ISBN 0-87353-594-4
1. Mathematics—Study and teaching—United States—Evaluation.
2. Mathematical ability—Testing. I. Title.
    QA13.R636 2006
    510.71—dc22

                                                                    2006016653

The National Council of Teachers of Mathematics is a public voice of mathematics education,
providing vision, leadership, and professional development to support teachers in ensuring
mathematics learning of the highest quality for all students.

Printed in the United States of America

CONTENTS

PREFACE

IN ITS FINAL report to the NCTM Board of Directors in September 2002, the Assessment Task Force, chaired by Diane Briars, recommended that the Council create materials to help its members better understand the basic ideas of mathematics assessment. To increase their shelf life, these materials were to avoid political and policy concerns that might date them. Instead, they were to be concise reference materials, written in not-too-technical language, that could be used by mathematics teachers, school and district administrators, parents, and policymakers to better understand the language and concepts used to design, conduct, and interpret information from classroom and large-scale assessments of students' ever-changing knowledge of mathematics.

This booklet grows out of the task force's recommendation. It is organized in two parts. Part 1 focuses on the language of mathematics assessment. In it, we define important terms like *standard, rubric, score, grade, test, reliability, validity, bias, formative, summative,* and *achievement.* We also outline unifying concepts, including ideas about the discipline of mathematics and how it is learned. In Part 2, we apply these terms and concepts to a discussion of standardized tests, the most common of the large-scale assessments that have come to dominate the educational landscape.

This booklet owes its existence to many people. Ann Shannon reviewed early versions, arranged for outside reviews, and, along with Norm Webb (a member of the Assessment Task Force), Patricia Ann Kenney, Jim Hirstein, and Harry Tunis, spent two days fleshing out the goals and overall structure of the document. Howard Everson provided a very helpful review of an early version of Part 2. Many mathematics educators across the country offered feedback during a series of presentations at regional and national conferences. Johnny Lott, president of NCTM when this project began, provided support and encouragement throughout. The current NCTM president, Cathy Seeley, and the current Board of Directors, made sure the project was completed. Any errors, of course, are the responsibility of the author.

PART 1

The Language of Mathematics Assessment: Concepts and Terms

> For one word a man is often deemed to be wise, and for one word he is often deemed to be foolish. We should indeed be careful what we say.
>
> —*Confucius*

Vignette:
The Parent Conference

For the umpteenth time this evening, Ms. Thompson summarized one line of her already chockful grade book for the parent of one of her students. "So, if I had to give Sarah a grade today, it would be a B."

Sarah sat quietly as her mother asked, "Sarah has been a little frustrated with math lately. She said something about the 'rubric' for the class, and I have to admit that I didn't know what she was talking about."

"Well, this rubric is how I grade the assessments." Ms. Thompson lifted a copy off the stack she had run off for the evening. "For example, on this assessment Sarah got a 3, which means she 'showed evidence of understanding, with some minor errors.' The highest score possible is 5."

"So this is like partial credit?"

"Well, it's similar."

Sarah's mother was still looking down at the page in the grade book as Ms. Thompson continued. "And as you can see here, Sarah has already met several of the district's Standards for seventh grade."

Sarah's mom nodded her head, and then asked, "How many of these Standards will Sarah need to meet to get an A?"

"Well, these are actually two different things. Sarah's grade is based on the assessments I make up, and the Standards get checked off according to the Standards assessments we give to all seventh graders. They are just like the questions on the SAP test." (Sarah's mom is all-too-familiar with the acronym for the State Assessment Program tests.)

"But if she meets all these Standards, then she'll move on to eighth-grade algebra?"

"Well, yes, if she passes my class."

"Won't she pass your class if she meets all the Standards?"

"Well, the grade in my class is not the same thing...."

Introduction

One word, *assessment*, has come to dominate the increasingly politicized language of mathematics education. Calls for changes in mathematics teaching practices include recommendations for more "authentic" classroom assessment of students' mathematical "understanding." State and national policymakers use data from "large scale, high stakes" assessments to hold students, teachers, schools, and districts "accountable" to meeting high "standards." It is vitally important for students, teachers, parents, and policymakers to be able to talk to one another about assessment. But for these conversations to be meaningful and productive, we need to share a commonly understood language. The *words* of assessment—words like *standard, rubric, score, grade, test, reliability, validity, bias, formative, summative, achievement,* and many others—must accurately convey the *ideas* of assessment. In this book, we propose definitions for many of the important words of mathematics assessment. To "define" is to give meaning to, to clarify, to make more precise. But some of the words of assessment, like the ambiguous ink blots of a Rorschach test, mean different things to different people. What is a standard? Other words are linked to each other as either-or dichotomies, often oversimplifying and misrepresenting their meaning. Are assessments either formative or summative? In our mathematical world, precise definitions underpin the structures we build. So it makes sense for us, as mathematics educators, to try to offer clear and unambiguous definitions of the terms of mathematics assessment.

We want this list of terms to be more than just another alphabetical glossary. (See Bracey 2000; American Educational Research Association, American Psychological Association, and National Council on Measurement in Education 1999; and National Council of Teachers of Mathematics [NCTM] 1995 for three such lists.) So we have organized the 32 formal definitions and 48 other important terms in this book into three sections. Following is a quick overview of these sections and some of the questions they tackle:

- Starting Points: What is mathematics assessment? What are intelligence, aptitude, and achievement? What are standards? What is error?

- Big Ideas: What are reliability, validity, and fairness? What are formative and summative assessments? Alternative, authentic, and performance assessments?

- Doing Assessment: What are standardized, norm-referenced, standards-referenced tests? What are scores, scoring rubrics, scaled scores, and cut scores? What are grades?

So, we have organized our definitions around the central ideas of assessment and suggested ways in which these words might be used to communicate these ideas. These ideas apply at all scales of mathematics assessment, from interviews with individual students to teacher-made classroom tests to large-scale state or national assessments.

Starting Points

What Is Mathematics Assessment?

> **Definition 1:** *Mathematics assessment* is the process of making inferences about the learning and teaching of mathematics by collecting and interpreting necessarily indirect and incomplete evidence.

In mathematics classrooms, teachers want to know which of their students have learned the important ideas, skills, strategies, and dispositions at the heart of a lesson or unit. Teachers also want to know the difficulties their students are having, when working independently and with others, so that they can fully evaluate their own teaching and thoughtfully prepare subsequent lessons. And teachers want to be able to track students' learning and the effectiveness of their teaching over an entire school year. District or state policymakers want to know if students are achieving at levels that warrant promotion or graduation or if programs are effectively meeting their intended goals. In each of these situations, *evidence*—students' written responses to a wide range of mathematical tasks as well as their oral interactions among themselves or the discussions between students and teachers—is used to make *inferences* about students' developing mathematical knowledge and about the effects of instruction on learning.

The definition of *mathematics assessment* is, itself, distinctly mathematical; it makes use of important ideas from measurement and statistics. Gathering assessment evidence is, at its heart, indirect measurement of complex *constructs* like "understanding place value" or "solving problems using proportional reasoning."

> **Definition 2:** A *construct* is a mathematical concept or set of concepts learned by students. Mathematics assessment is designed to gather evidence about constructs.

Any measurements include the background noise of *error*, and the indirect measurements of mathematics assessment are subject to errors of many kinds. Important statistical ideas and techniques help us understand and minimize this noise so that we can make meaningful inferences.

> **Definition 3:** We define two unavoidable types of assessment error. *Measurement error* is due to the lack of complete precision of the assessment process. *Sampling error* results from the differences between a sample and the population from which it is drawn.

Every assessment inference is merely an estimate of knowledge, achievement, or growth. *Random errors* are just as likely to overestimate as to underestimate the true (but unknowable) value of the construct. Measurements that are more likely to err in one direction than the other produce *systematic errors*. In statistics, *samples* are chosen to represent a larger and often inaccessible population. These samples are never perfectly representative, and any inferences will be subject to *sampling error*. In assessment, the items on a quiz or test are samples of the set of possible items, and the students in a middle school are samples from the pool of all possible middle school students.

Assessment of What?

What is mathematics? What does it mean to know and do mathematics? How do students learn mathematics? It makes little sense for a teacher or test developer to try to collect evidence and make inferences without first thinking carefully about the nature of the discipline of mathematics and how students come to know it.

In *Knowing What Students Know,* the National Research Council (2001) depicts assessment as a triangle (fig. 1). The three vertices of this triangle highlight that mathematics assessment is about observing and interpreting evidence *about learning.* We would add that, for us, the bottom vertex of this triangle is about *mathematics learning.*

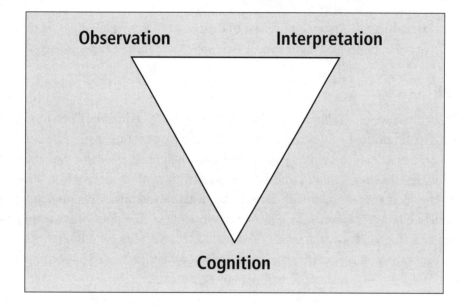

Fig. 1. The assessment triangle

On the one hand, mathematics might be construed as a set of procedures, tools, and techniques that can be used to quickly and accurately find solutions to specific classes of problems. Learning this mathematics might be understood as the steady accrual by practice of these techniques and skills. In this instance, students should be assessed using evidence that they can recall these tools and techniques in the appropriate circumstances and then use them quickly and efficiently.

On the other hand, mathematics might be viewed, as portrayed in *Principles and Standards for School Mathematics* (NCTM 2000), as a connected and useful set of big ideas about number, shape, and data, along with ways of using these ideas to solve problems and develop new ideas. Learning this mathematics might be seen as a socially supported process through which learners bring prior knowledge to bear to construct new knowledge. In this instance, students should be assessed using evidence that shows that they, working alone and with others, can bring mathematical ideas to bear to solve problems and to find and generalize quantitative relationships.

Not surprisingly, we embrace the second of these views of mathematics and learning. However, no matter what views you hold, no discussion of assessment makes sense without explicitly including assumptions and expectations about mathematics and how it is learned (Shepard 1999). One way to say this is to call for assessment to be *aligned* with curriculum and instruction.

> **Definition 4:** *Alignment* is used to describe the extent to which mathematics curriculum, instruction, and assessment are mutually supportive.

Intelligence

The construct of *intelligence* permeates mathematics education, even today. In the early years of the twentieth century, intelligence was thought to be a single, innate characteristic of individual people, like their height or eye color. Some people had more intelligence; others had less. And, like height, intelligence was assumed to follow the "bell-shaped curve" of the normal distribution: many people have close to average intelligence, a few have very high intelligence, and a few have very low intelligence (fig. 2). The terms *ability* and *aptitude* have been used interchangeably to represent the same idea. The intelligence tests of the time were designed to locate people on the bell-shaped curve of innate intelligence.

> **Definition 5:** *Intelligence Quotient*, or IQ, was computed by dividing a person's intellectual age—determined by an intelligence test—by her mental age, and then multiplying the result by 100.

The echoes of this understanding of intelligence are heard today in comments like "some people can do math, but some cannot," and in practices like distributing classroom grades so that only a few students are given A's, whereas "average" students are given C's.

Our position is somewhat different. Assessment that embodies both the dynamic discipline of mathematics described in *Principles and Standards* and what we know today about how students come to know this discipline can support a

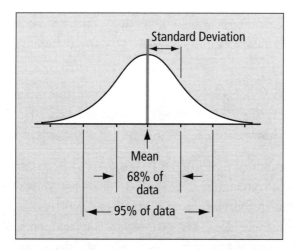

Fig. 2. The normal distribution and some of its features

mathematics "learning culture" in classrooms, schools, and communities (Shepard 1999). Assessment supports this learning culture by determining what students can do at any point in time (their levels of *achievement*), by charting the growth in students' knowledge over time, and by providing constructive and supportive feedback. There is no doubt that some students are more talented mathematically than others, in the same way that some students are more talented artistically, musically, or athletically than others. And just as with the arts or sports, talent can be cultivated by sound instruction. We presume that *all* students have sufficient mathematical talent, when nurtured by sound instruction (what some call *developed abilities*), to meet the expectations of a high-quality school mathematics program.

What Are Standards?

Ask five people what they mean by "standards" and you will get six different answers. We will not use the word *standard* alone. Instead, we will make the distinction between content standards and performance standards.

> **Definition 6:** *Content standards* are the mathematical strands that compose the school mathematics curriculum.

In *Principles and Standards for School Mathematics*, NCTM describes a school mathematics curriculum organized around these big ideas: number and operations, algebra, geometry, measurement, data analysis and probability, problem solving, reasoning and proof, communication, connections, and representation. These content standards are the elements of mathematics we want students to learn about in school.[1]

> **Definition 7:** *Performance standards* are the achievement expectations to which students are held. Performance standards specify what students are expected to know about each of the content standards at specific times.

The National Assessment of Educational Progress (NAEP) specifies three levels of performance—Basic, Proficient, and Advanced—at each of the three grade levels at which NAEP is administered. For example, Proficient eighth graders should "be able to conjecture, defend their ideas, and give supporting examples. They should understand the connections between fractions, percents, decimals, and other mathematical topics such as algebra and functions." In addition, "Quantity and spatial relationships in problem solving and reasoning should be familiar to them, and they should be able to convey underlying reasoning skills beyond the level of arithmetic."[2] Whether we are dealing with a classroom quiz or a state-level test, performance standards describe what we expect students to be able to do with particular mathematics ideas and concepts.

So in other words, content standards portray the mathematical landscape, and performance standards describe what students should know of this landscape at specific times. The term *mastery* is often used to denote a high standard of performance. However, the term might also be interpreted as signifying "complete" knowledge of some concept or skill. To avoid this interpretation, and to emphasize that mathematics concepts and skills are complex and virtually limitless in breadth and depth, we will avoid using the term *mastery*.

We conclude this section by defining several terms that arise naturally when talking about standards.

> **Definition 8:** The term *benchmark* derives from the practice of crafts people who cut notches into their workbenches to be used to place materials for consistent cutting. In assessment, *benchmarks* are descriptions or models

---

1. The last five of these standards are called Process Standards in *Principles and Standards for School Mathematics.* We include them as examples of content standards because for each of them we can set performance expectations that grow over time—as we can, for example, for algebra or geometry.

2. The full set of performance standards for NAEP, also known as "the nation's report card," are available online at nces.ed.gov/nationsreportcard/mathematics/achieveall.asp.

of specific performance standards. The highest benchmark is an *exemplar*, a model of outstanding performance. An *anchor paper* is a sample of a student's work that has met a particular benchmark.

The following statement on assessment is from *Principles and Standards for School Mathematics* (NCTM 2000, p. 22):

The Assessment Principle: Assessment should support the learning of important mathematics and furnish useful information to both teachers and students.

The following statements on assessment are from *Assessment Standards for School Mathematics* (NCTM 1995):

Assessment should
- reflect the mathematics that all students need to know and be able to do (p. 11);
- enhance mathematics learning (p. 13);
- promote equity (p. 15);
- be an open process (p. 17);
- promote valid inferences about mathematics learning (p. 19);
- be a coherent process (p. 21).

The Big Ideas: Reliability, Validity, and Fairness

Reliability, validity, and fairness are the three pillars of quality that support any mathematics assessment.

Definition 9: Assessment is *reliable* if it produces accurate and consistent evidence. Reliability is a description of the precision of assessment.

If different scorers or raters agree on the amount and quality of the evidence gathered, then the assessment process is said to have *inter-rater reliability*. If repeating the assessment process produces similar evidence, then assessment has *test-retest reliability*. In large-scale assessment, a *reliability coefficient* is a measure of the correlation among scores assigned by different scorers or among scores on repeated administrations of the test.

> **Definition 10:** *Valid* uses of assessment evidence produce meaningful inferences about students' mathematical knowledge. Valid inferences are well supported by the amount and quality of the evidence and by what we know about how students know and do mathematics.

That is, the validity of assessment is a function of the uses made of the information. If assessment information is being used to determine how much students know about mathematics, then we should wonder about the *content validity* or *construct validity* of the assessment. Classroom tests must have high content validity if the evidence they furnish is to be useful for supporting future learning and instruction. College entrance exams like the SAT and ACT are designed to predict students' success in their first year of college. How well the tests do this is a measure of their *predictive validity*. Given the high stakes for students, graduation or promotion tests must have high *consequential validity*.

> **Definition 11:** The *stakes* of an assessment refer to the consequences of inferences made.

Tests used for promotion, graduation, or college entrance are examples of assessments with *high stakes* for individual students. Tests that are used to rate a program or school have high stakes for that program or school (and might, indirectly, have high stakes for the students as well). A single short quiz given in class would have *low stakes* if it was only one of many opportunities for the students in that class to provide evidence of what they know.

> **Definition 12:** Assessment is *fair* if the assessment tasks are not biased, if all students have had equal opportunities to learn the content being assessed, and if all students are treated equally by the assessment process. Unfair mathematics assessment produces inaccurate inferences about the mathematics knowledge of a particular group of students.

> **Definition 13:** An assessment task is *biased* if it produces evidence with systematic errors.

The following example will help illustrate the big assessment ideas of reliability, validity, and fairness, and how interconnected these ideas are.

Item 1:	**Item 2:**
$1\frac{3}{4} \div \frac{1}{2} =$ (a) $\frac{7}{8}$ (b) $\frac{7}{4}$ (c) $3\frac{1}{2}$ (d) $3\frac{1}{4}$	Find the value of the expression $$1\frac{3}{4} \div \frac{1}{2}$$ and then describe a mathematical problem for which you would have to find the value of this expression to solve the problem.

Each of these items is designed to assess students' knowledge of the division of fractions. On Item 1, only five responses are possible: the correct answer (c), one of the three incorrect answers, or no response (also an incorrect answer). Different scorers will have no trouble agreeing about the correctness of the answer a student gives. This item can be scored reliably.

Now, imagine this item could be posed to the same student over and over, without the student remembering from time to time. Occasionally, the student might make some careless arithmetic error or read the problem incorrectly. So a student might not respond the same way each time. It is very likely, however, that she will respond the same way almost every time. Next, imagine asking a large group of students to respond to this item, and then at some later time (long enough for them not to remember the first time) asking them again. There will be a high correlation between these two sets of answers. For each of these reasons, this item is highly reliable.

Item 2, however, might produce a wide range of responses from students. For different scorers to agree on the correctness of an answer, they would have to have clear guidelines for assigning scores. Even with a very specific set of clear guidelines, scorers will have to make judgments about the evidence in the students' answers. Some practice would be needed to help scorers make these judgments in agreed-on ways. If these criteria have been met, we could expect reliable evidence from this item as well.

But what does a correct response to Item 1 tell us? What is it evidence of? We could infer from this limited evidence that this student knows how to divide fractions. However, she might have simply guessed the correct answer. So this inference would have limited validity for this purpose. If the student were asked five questions similar to this one and she consistently responded correctly, then this additional, more reliable evidence could be used to make a somewhat more valid inference about this student's knowledge of a procedure for dividing fractions. However, because selecting the correct answer provides no evidence of the procedure itself, this inference would not have high validity.

A correct response to Item 2 might look like this:

$$\frac{7}{4} - \frac{2}{4} = \frac{5}{4}$$

$$\frac{5}{4} - \frac{2}{4} = \frac{3}{4} \qquad 3 \text{ and } \frac{\frac{1}{4}}{\frac{1}{2}} = 3\frac{1}{2} \qquad \text{If I have a jar with } 1\frac{3}{4} \text{ cups of sugar in it,}$$

and I scoop out 1/2 cup at a time, how many scoops can I get?

$$\frac{3}{4} - \frac{2}{4} = \frac{1}{4}$$

We might infer from this response, which does provide evidence of a procedure, that the student knows a method for dividing fractions, that this method is based on a repeated-subtraction model of division, and that the student has some sense of when we would need to divide fractions. As before, consistent responses to several items like this would improve the reliability of the evidence and the validity of this inference.

Item 1 has higher reliability than Item 2, so some might argue that the assessment of students' knowledge of the division of fractions should, to increase its reliability, be based solely on items like this one. But inferences about students' understanding of the division of fractions would actually be more valid if they were based on the somewhat less reliable evidence from items like Item 2.

Now imagine that these two items are given to students in two classes. The students in one class do much better on these items than the students in the other. How might this evidence be used? Some inferences include the following:

- The students in one class know more about the division of fractions, on average, than the students in the other class.

- The students in one class have a better teacher than the students in the other class.

- The students in one class are more capable than the students in the other class.

Although students' responses to these items provide some evidence of what the students know, they say nothing about when or where these students learned this. Without other evidence, the last two of these inferences would be invalid. Even the first inference might be suspect. Imagine, for example, that one class never covered the unit on the division of fractions, whereas the other class spent considerable time practicing items just like these. What if one class was given only two minutes to respond to the questions, but the other class got to take the items home? In each of these situations, the unfairness of the assessment would undermine the validity of any inferences. What if one class has a large number of students for whom English is not their first language? This assessment would be unfair to them, and each of these inferences would have little validity because of the facility with the English language needed to understand and respond correctly to the second item.

For assessment to be valid, it must be reliable and fair. But reliability and fairness do not ensure validity. And in some instances, increasing the reliability of assessment might actually reduce the richness of the evidence, thereby decreasing the validity of inferences.

> **Definition 14:** *Authentic assessment* uses reliable evidence to make valid inferences.

The terms *authentic assessment* and *performance assessment* have been used in mathematics to describe assessment in real-world, applied contexts. We will not use these terms. A task like Item 1 above is authentic if the goal is to find out if a student can divide one fraction by another. In mathematics, well-aligned, reliable assessment used for valid purposes will be authentic.

The term *alternative assessment* in mathematics has been used to refer to assessment methods that are alternatives to the familiar quizzes and tests. Some have used the term to denote preferred, more meaningful, assessment methods as contrasted with less meaningful traditional assessment. We will treat the full range of assessment methods—from traditionally used quizzes and tests to newer methods like portfolios and projects—as having value, as long as they are authentic.

The terms *formative* and *summative* assessment have been in wide use since the 1970s. Written quizzes and the informal assessment of students' daily work, when used by teachers to give their students meaningful feedback and to plan subsequent lessons, would be examples of formative assessment. Final exams and most large-scale assessments would be examples of summative assessment.

Definition 15: *Formative assessment* is diagnostic; the evidence is used to guide subsequent instruction and support continued learning.

Definition 16: *Summative assessment* offers evidence used to make inferences about what students have achieved—what they know and are able to do—at a specific point in time.

These terms highlight the *placement* of assessments in the instructional program and the different *roles* they play. But these terms are not mutually exclusive. Most assessment activities have both formative and summative features. An end-of-unit final exam can inform individual students about how well they learned the content in the unit and what is left to learn, and it can inform the teacher about how well her instruction accomplished its goals and what she should do next. A state graduation exam can inform school administrators about whether students have met established performance standards for graduation. Therefore, all assessment is *informative* (Bass and Glazer 2004), as long as the evidence is reliable and the uses are valid.

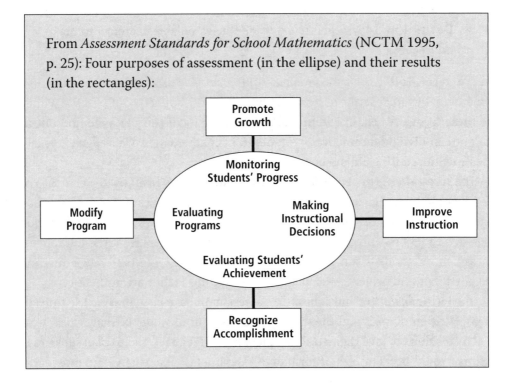

From *Assessment Standards for School Mathematics* (NCTM 1995, p. 25): Four purposes of assessment (in the ellipse) and their results (in the rectangles):

Doing Assessment:
Gathering and Using Evidence

The nuts and bolts of mathematics assessment include ways to collect evidence of students' understanding, the many types of inferences, and how these inferences are reported.

> **Definition 17:** A *standardized test* is administered under identical conditions for all test takers. Any test can be standardized if all students are given the same or equated test questions, if they have the same access to resources, if they are given the same directions and the same amount of time to complete the test, and if their work is scored the same.

When a teacher gives the same exam to students in different classes taking the same course, she might try to standardize the test by giving all the classes the same amount of time and the same access to notes, the text, and calculators. Large-scale assessment administrators are provided with specific agendas and scripts to ensure that all students are given the same instructions and resources.

> **Definition 18:** A *norm-referenced* test reports students' scores relative to those of a previously chosen and tested reference group. The mean score of examinees in the reference group is called the *norm.*

The SAT Reasoning Test in Mathematics is a norm-referenced test. The reference group consists of college-intending students chosen so as to be representative of the diverse high school student population. The mean score of this group—the norm—is assigned a scale score of 500. Any student who takes the SAT and produces a raw score on this test equal to the norm will also score 500.

> **Definition 19:** A *standards-referenced* test reports scores based on predetermined performance standards. The term *criterion-referenced* test has been used to mean the same thing.

Certification tests, such as the graduation tests used by many states, are often standards-referenced. Performance standards for graduation are set prior to giving the test, and students' performances are held up to this standard. The National Assessment of Educational Progress (NAEP), which rates students' performance as Basic, Proficient, or Advanced based on previously defined performance standards, is another example of a standards-referenced test.

All assessment, whether standards-based or norm-referenced, whether standardized or not, begins with the posing of tasks.

Definition 20: *Tasks, items,* and *prompts* are specific mathematical problems and questions designed to elicit assessment evidence.

Definition 21: Types of assessment tasks:
- *Closed Tasks*—Tasks that have a single path to a single correct answer
- *Open-Middled Tasks*—Tasks that have multiple paths to a single correct answer
- *Open-Ended Tasks*—Tasks with several or many correct answers
- *Projects*—Extended open-ended tasks
- *On-Demand Assessment*—Tasks designed and posed to students at particular times by teachers or test developers
- *Portfolios*—Evidence of a student's learning or achievement selected and offered by the student herself

Definition 22: Formats of assessment tasks:
- *Selected-Response Tasks*—Students choose from a list of possible responses. Multiple-choice, true-false, and matching tasks are all selected-response tasks.
- *Constructed-Response Tasks*—Students create their own response. Short constructed responses might include just numerical answers. Extended constructed-response tasks might ask students to show all their work or explain why their solutions make sense.

Once evidence is gathered, it has to be recorded and interpreted. This is the first level of inference.

Definition 23: A *score* is a number, letter, or other symbol used to denote the quality of evidence present in a student's response to an assessment task as compared to a set of guidelines or performance standards. *Scoring* is the process of assigning scores.

Definition 24: In mathematics assessment, a *rubric* is the set of rules for scoring students' work on constructed-response tasks. *Generic rubrics* provide general guidelines that may be applied to a wide variety of tasks. *Specific rubrics* are for use with specific tasks.

The word *rubric* is derived from the Latin word "rubrica," which means red. Rubrics are the specific rules for conducting church services, written in red in the margins of church texts.

Definition 25: A *holistic score* is a single score based on the overall quality of the evidence provided by a student's response.

Definition 26: *Analytic scoring* of a student's performance on an assessment item begins by identifying two or more aspects or dimensions of that performance to be assessed separately. A score is then assigned for each of these aspects or dimensions.

Figure 3 gives an example of an open-middled, constructed-response task, along with specific holistic and analytic scoring rubrics (Bush and Greer 1999, pp. 91–92).

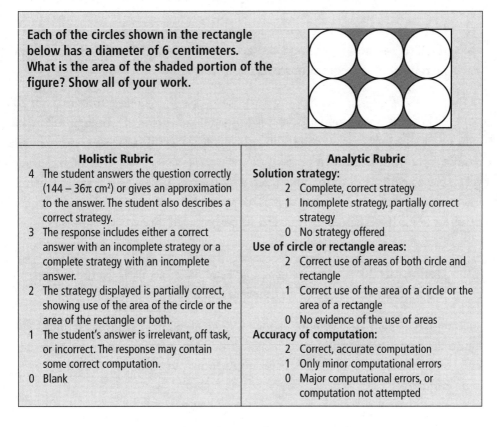

Each of the circles shown in the rectangle below has a diameter of 6 centimeters. What is the area of the shaded portion of the figure? Show all of your work.

Holistic Rubric	Analytic Rubric
4 The student answers the question correctly $(144 - 36\pi$ cm^2) or gives an approximation to the answer. The student also describes a correct strategy.	**Solution strategy:** 2 Complete, correct strategy 1 Incomplete strategy, partially correct strategy 0 No strategy offered
3 The response includes either a correct answer with an incomplete strategy or a complete strategy with an incomplete answer.	**Use of circle or rectangle areas:** 2 Correct use of areas of both circle and rectangle 1 Correct use of the area of a circle or the area of a rectangle 0 No evidence of the use of areas
2 The strategy displayed is partially correct, showing use of the area of the circle or the area of the rectangle or both.	**Accuracy of computation:** 2 Correct, accurate computation 1 Only minor computational errors
1 The student's answer is irrelevant, off task, or incorrect. The response may contain some correct computation.	0 Major computational errors, or computation not attempted
0 Blank	

Fig. 3. A task with specific scoring rubrics

A student's *raw score* is often just a count of the number of correct items. Many different types of scores are *derived* from the raw score. Percentile scores are often used on classroom quizzes and tests; a raw score of 15 correct out of 20 might lead to a *derived score* of 75 percent. On many large-scale assessments, derived scores are norm-referenced, that is, based on the relative ranking of a student's raw score when compared to some reference group. An SAT Mathematics Reasoning Test score of 500 is a derived score based on a raw score equal to the average raw score of the students in a previously chosen, nationally representative comparison group of college-intending students.

A *grade-equivalent score* is another example of a derived score. If a sixth grader receives a mathematics grade-equivalent score of 6.5 on a norm-referenced test like the Iowa Test of Basic Skills (ITBS), this means she had a raw score equal to the raw score of the average sixth grader in the norm-reference group, who was given the test in the middle of the school year. A grade-equivalent score of 7.5 would correspond to the performance of the average seventh grader *on this sixth-grade test.*

> **Definition 27:** A *scale* is a measurement dimension. *Scaled scores* are derived scores. Raw scores on a test are transformed arithmetically so they can be reported on a common scale.

The SAT Mathematics Reasoning Test uses a scale of whole numbers from 200 to 800, and the ACT Mathematics test is reported on a scale of whole numbers between 1 and 36. Many state accountability tests report a scale score for each student. A common scale is used to report students' performances on each of the grade-level tests, so scores are comparable from year to year. When test-design principles known as Item Response Theory are used, students' performances can be located on this scale on the basis of the pattern of correct and incorrect responses on the test.

> **Definition 28:** Test score *equating* establishes a relationship that permits the comparison of scores on different tests.

Some large-scale assessments use what are called *parallel forms,* which might include the same items in different order, some identical items, or even two completely different sets of items. In each example, however, scores are equated so they can be compared.

> **Definition 29:** A *gain score* is the difference between a student's scores on the same or equated tests at two different points in time.

18

Gain scores are used to show growth over time. For gain scores to be valid, the two tests' scores must be reported on a common scale.

> **Definition 30:** A *cut score* is a point on a scoring scale where performance is judged to move from one level to the next.

The score set by a teacher for passing a classroom test is one example of a cut score. Two types of cut scores are used in large-scale assessments. Certification tests like graduation tests set a single cut score: if your score is higher than the cut score, you graduate. Standards-referenced tests that report performance levels set a series of cut scores. On the National Assessment of Educational Progress, for example, one cut score marks the transition from Basic to Proficient performance, and a higher cut score divides Proficient and Advanced performance.

> **Definition 31:** A *grade* is a number, letter, or other symbol used to summarize how the body of assessment evidence gathered for a student up to a point in time compares to the set of expectations for the student at that time. Grading is the process of assigning grades.

Here is an example to illustrate the difference between scoring and grading. A gymnast might receive a score of 4.8 on a particular routine. Judges determine this score by holding the gymnast's routine up against a specific set of guidelines, including the number and quality of specific moves of varying difficulty performed during the routine. (Several judges' scores are combined, in order to improve the score's reliability.) However, this score of 4.8 might result in a grade of A—for a seven-year-old novice gymnast—or a grade of F—for an Olympic-caliber gymnast—because of the vastly different expectations for these two performers at the time of the performance (Wiggins 1998).

> **Definition 32:** *Evaluation* is the process of using judgment to determine the value of assessment evidence. Grading is one example of evaluation.

Concluding Comments

Slovenly language corrodes the mind.

—John Quincy Adams

Our goal with this portion of the book has been to convey the important ideas of mathematics assessment through the words we use to talk about this politically charged but essential component of mathematics teaching and learning. We use these terms throughout this booklet, whether focusing on the assessment done by teachers with their own students in their mathematics classrooms or dealing, in not-too-technical terms, with the important ideas of the science of *psychometrics*.

Many of the words in this book mean different things to different people and, therefore, convey little. A "slovenly language" discourages discussion. But all of us who have a stake in the broad success of school mathematics education have the responsibility to engage one another in meaningful discussion about assessment. Our hope is that the definitions and uses we have proposed here will sharpen the meanings of the words of assessment—and the ideas they represent—to encourage meaningful talk among teachers, administrators, parents, policymakers, and our students.

PART 2

Understanding Large-Scale Assessment

> Get your facts first, and then you can distort them as
> much as you please.
>
> *—Mark Twain*

Large-scale assessments are prominent and imposing features of today's educational landscape. As these assessments grow in number and influence, the controversy surrounding their uses grows as well.

Introduction

What are large-scale assessments? What are standardized tests? How are these tests conceived and constructed? How are they administered and scored? How are their results reported? What are scale scores, grade equivalent scores, cut scores? How are test scores equated? How are the results of these tests interpreted and used, and how are they misinterpreted and misused? The answers to these questions have serious implications for the students these assessments are ultimately designed to serve. This booklet will offer some answers—some of the facts of large-scale assessment—so that teachers, school and district administrators, and other stakeholders might draw their own conclusions about the proper roles for these assessments in the mathematics education of students.

Mathematics assessment is the process of making inferences about the learning or teaching of mathematics by collecting and interpreting necessarily indirect and incomplete evidence. In classrooms, teachers make inferences about their own students' knowledge using evidence they collect from quizzes and tests; from projects, journals, and portfolios; and from daily observations of their students doing mathematics. Teachers can continually refine the inferences they make by aligning their assessments with their taught curriculum; by giving increased weight to evidence of important understandings; and by building a diverse body of evidence, from a variety of sources, bit by bit over an entire school year.

In contrast, large-scale assessments are removed from the specific curriculum and instructional context of any particular classroom. These assessments may take many forms: for example, tests, portfolio systems, and progress maps. But most large-scale assessments are tests—achievement tests, placement tests, or admissions tests—built from large collections of items in a variety of formats ("selected response" or "forced choice" items, and "free response" or "constructed response" items). These tests are one-shot assessment "events," administered under standardized conditions of time, place, and available resources. They are scored, and these scores are used, individually or together with other assessment information, to make a wide variety of educational decisions. These decisions can have great consequences for students and the schools they attend.

Tests vary widely in quality: they may be scored incorrectly, and the pressure to score well on high-stakes tests might lead to cheating. These problems produce useless test information and pose great risks for students and schools. All consumers of test information must be on guard against such problems as these. But even carefully constructed, fairly administered, and accurately scored tests provide information that is difficult to interpret. In this booklet we will focus on well-designed tests, the information they furnish, and the utility and limits of this information.

Starting Points

The Three Big Ideas of Assessment

Reliability, validity, and fairness are the three pillars of quality that support any mathematics assessment.

Reliability

Assessment is *reliable* if it produces accurate and consistent evidence. Reliability is a description of the precision of assessment. If different scorers or raters agree on the amount and quality of the evidence gathered, then the assessment process is said to have *interrater reliability*. If repeating the assessment process produces similar evidence, then assessment has *test-retest reliability*. In large-scale assessment, a *reliability coefficient* is a measure of the correlation among scores assigned by different scorers, or among scores on repeated administrations of the test.

Validity

Valid uses of assessment evidence produce meaningful inferences about students' mathematical knowledge. Valid inferences are well supported by the amount and quality of the evidence and by what we know about how students know and do mathematics.

So, the validity of assessment is a function of the uses made of the information. If assessment information is being used to determine how much students know about mathematics, then we should wonder about the *content validity* or *construct validity* of the assessment. Classroom tests must have high content validity if the evidence they provide is to be useful for supporting future learning and instruction. College entrance exams like the SAT and ACT are designed to predict students' success in their first year of college. How well the tests do this is a measure of their *predictive validity*. Given the high stakes for students, graduation or promotion tests must have high *consequential validity*.

Fairness

Assessment is *fair* if the assessment tasks are not biased, if all students have had equal opportunities to learn the content being assessed, and if all students are treated equally by the assessment process. Unfair mathematics assessment produces inaccurate inferences about the mathematics knowledge of a particular group of students. An assessment task is *biased* if it produces evidence with systematic errors. (We discuss error in more detail below.)

These three ideas are inextricably connected. Validity requires reliability, but it does not guarantee it; information cannot be used meaningfully if it is inaccurate, but even accurate information can be misused. Fairness requires both reliability and validity.

Recurring Themes

Students' knowledge of mathematics is complex and always changing. We know this knowledge is there somewhere because we see students using it to do mathematics. The primary purpose of tests is to measure this knowledge, but these measurements cannot be done directly. Every test designer makes decisions about the mathematics content to be measured, and every test designer must deal with unavoidable errors when trying to measure what students know about that content. These are themes that run throughout this booklet.

Mathematics

Content. For test designers hoping to construct a test of, for example, students' knowledge of eighth-grade mathematics, the first question they face is, "What is eighth-grade mathematics?" The designers might answer this question by reviewing widely used texts or conducting a national survey of curriculum topics. The picture of eighth-grade mathematics that emerges from this approach will be a "common denominator" list of topics that spans all texts and curriculum guides. The designers would include on their test one or two questions from each of these topics. A student's responses to this sample of all possible questions would offer evidence from which inferences might be made about her knowledge of this broadly defined domain. This approach to defining mathematics content and then building a test is called *domain sampling*.

Eighth-grade mathematics is defined for some test designers by a set of state or district standards. These standards describe mathematical topics and their relative importance to the state or district, as well as outlining important processes like problem solving, reasoning, and communication. The designers would then build a test containing several items keyed to each of these standards (an approach known as *standards-based sampling*). A student's responses to the items on this test would provide evidence that would be used to make inferences about whether or not she has met these standards.

Difficulty. What makes a test or test item difficult? To illustrate the subtlety of this question, we offer the following graph (see fig. 4), with axes that represent two of the many dimensions of item difficulty: cognitive complexity and content level.

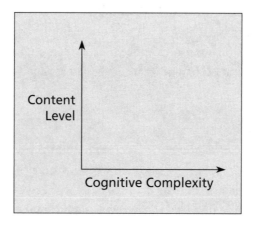

Fig. 4. Two dimensions of difficulty

To explain what these dimensions are and how they interact to determine the difficulty of a test item, we will analyze two sample test items.

Item 1[3]

A crate contains 63 oranges, 47 apples, and 95 pears. If one more of each type of fruit were added to the crate, each of the three types of fruit could be divided equally among a group of people. What is the greatest possible number of people in such a group?

(A) 8   (B) 12   (C) 15   (D) 16   (E) 32

To answer Item 1 correctly, students might add 1 to each of the three numbers to get 64, 48, and 96, and then note that 16 is the largest of the choices that divides each of these numbers evenly. The mathematical content of this item is covered in middle school, but several mathematical steps, and some close reading, are required to answer the question correctly. With relatively high cognitive complexity but low content level, this item might be plotted in the lower-right region of the graph in figure 4.

Item 2

What is the value of $\cos\left(\dfrac{\pi}{6}\right)$?

(A) $\dfrac{1}{2}$ (B) $\sqrt{3}$ (C) $\dfrac{\sqrt{3}}{2}$ (D) $\sqrt{2}$ (E) $\dfrac{\sqrt{2}}{2}$

Item 2, however, taps content—the cosine function and angles expressed in radians—not usually covered until a class in trigonometry. Students could answer this question correctly simply by recalling that $\cos(\pi/6) = \sqrt{3}/2$. This item, with its high-level content but low-level complexity, might appear in the upper-left region of the graph in figure 4.

Which of these selected-response items is more difficult? Item 2 might be easy for a group of eleventh-grade trigonometry students but difficult for a group of

---

3. This item is taken from a full-length practice SAT Reasoning Test in Mathematics, available online at www.collegeboard.com/student/testing/sat/prep_one/test.html.

25

eighth graders. Also, the cognitive complexity of Item 1 might make it difficult even for eleventh graders.

We've chosen to highlight only two dimensions of difficulty in this discussion, using two items of the same type. Test items that do not give answer choices—and that ask for written explanations or justifications—might be placed much farther out on the cognitive complexity dimension. Students' performances on a test will depend both on how the content of the test is determined and on the difficulty of the items included on the test.

Error

In this section we introduce two types of error[4] that add uncertainty to interpretations of evidence from large-scale assessment: *measurement error* and *sampling error*.

Measurement error. Any measurement is subject to error. Even the most precise instruments are accurate only within certain limits. This is true even if the measurement is direct, such as in the measurement of an object's length with a ruler. The accuracy of any measurement of length will depend on the ruler, on the person using it, and on the shape and other physical characteristics of the object being measured. A person can reduce *random* errors by taking many measurements and then finding their average. However, if she holds the ruler with the zero mark in the wrong place each time she takes a measurement, she will create *systematic* error.

When assessing mathematical knowledge, measurement is complicated further because it is indirect. The "ruler"—the test—cannot simply be placed alongside a student's mathematical knowledge so that the result may be read. Mathematical knowledge is an inaccessible mental construct, and any test is a measurement instrument that produces evidence rife with error. Repeated administrations of the test (if that were possible) would likely produce somewhat different results. Students will never be perfectly consistent in their answers to a set of questions, and other factors unrelated to their knowledge are bound to affect their responses.

Sampling error. To assess a large group's position on any issue, pollsters select a sample of people from this population and ask them a set of questions. The accuracy of any inferences made will depend on how well the sample represents the population of interest and on the set of questions asked.

---

4. As we mentioned earlier, test items can be miskeyed or incorrectly scored, and scores can be lost or incorrectly reported. Although these are real problems that can have devastating consequences in a high-stakes testing environment, our use of the word *error* does not include these *mistakes*.

Similarly, several types of sampling introduce error in the results of a large-scale assessment and in the uses of these results. First, only a sample of all possible items is used on any test. Therefore, the choice of items introduces sampling error in the scores of individual students. Second, just as in a survey or poll, only samples of students might be selected for the assessment from the populations of interest. For example, the National Assessment of Educational Progress samples about 150,000 students—50,000 at each of the three grade levels 4, 8, and 12—to make claims about all U.S. students in these grade levels. Even with these large samples and even though a good deal of effort goes into selecting representative samples of students, there is still sampling error in any evidence gathered.

Here is a third, more subtle source of sampling error: the students in a school who take a state-level assessment are only a sample of all possible students who could have gone through the specific program offered by that school that year. Inferences about the quality of that program are subject to random error related to the size of the sample—small schools contain small samples with larger error—and to systematic error, because these are not randomly selected samples of students. (We will say more about this later.)

Choosing a Test

Imagine the following scenario: A school district's mathematics committee—a group of administrators, teachers, and parents—has been asked by the superintendent to select a mathematics test the district can use to assess its eighth graders. The district's accountability plan calls for including test data when—

- reporting what individual students know about the mathematics outlined in the state's mathematics standards;

- placing students in their ninth-grade classes;

- evaluating the mathematics curriculum and instruction at each of the district's twenty middle schools.

Educational systems of all sizes, from schools to districts to states, make decisions like these all the time, and many use—or are considering using—data from large-scale assessments. Using two hypothetical tests, we explore the important mathematical ideas this fictional school district must consider if it hopes to use test information to make these decisions in ways that are both meaningful and fair. In the sections that follow, and in a series of appendixes, we define many technical terms and discuss many issues usually provided by test developers in their technical manuals. (A list of these terms is included in an index.) We hope this short primer on *psychometrics*, the science of testing, will help nonspecialists make better use of these manuals.

The Tests

In practice, school districts have a wide range of tests from which to choose. To simplify our discussion, we will focus on two hypothetical tests. These are not actual tests with the names changed; rather, they possess features common to two different, and familiar, types of tests.

Test A
- A nationally norm-referenced test
- Content specifications based on domain sampling
- Contains multiple-choice and short, free-response items
- Reports three scores for each student: a national percentile rank, a grade equivalent score, and a scaled score based on the familiar SAT scale of 200–800

Test B
- A standards-based test, with content specifications based on the state's standards
- Contains multiple-choice and a variety of free-response items
- Reports two scores for each student: a scale score using a scale from 200 to 1000, and a performance level (either "Basic," "Developing," "Proficient," or "Advanced")

Which of these tests would best meet the stated needs of this school district? In the sections that follow, we will consider this question, one use at a time.

Proposed Use 1: What Do Students Know?

Using Test A

How well will student scores from the Test A, a test designed using the principles of Classical Test Theory (see Appendix A), convey what students know about eighth- grade mathematics? Imagine, for example, that a student obtains the following scores on this norm-referenced test:

- National Percentile Rank: 84
- Grade Equivalent Score: 9.5
- Scaled Score: 600

How are these scores determined? What do they mean? What evidence do they offer about what students know?

To derive national percentile ranks, grade equivalent scores, and scaled scores, the developers of this test do the following:

- Select a national norm reference group and give their test to the students in this group.

- Compare scores of all other students to the scores of the norm reference group.

The norm reference group. First, the test developers select a large random sample of U.S. eighth graders to take the test. Random sampling, carefully done, will produce a norm reference group representative of the country's eighth graders, subject to sampling error.

Once these students have been selected, the developers give them the test. The students' raw scores on the test—based on their correct and incorrect responses— are listed from lowest to highest so that the developers can assign a percentile rank to each raw score. For example, they would give a percentile rank of 65 to a raw score higher than 65 percent of the scores in this group.

Next, the developers compute the mean (average) and the standard deviation of this set of raw scores. These statistics are used to compute a *standardized score*, or z-score, for each raw score. The mean raw score has a z-score of 0, a raw score that is one standard deviation above the mean score is assigned a z-score of +1, and for a raw score two standard deviations below the mean, the z-score is −2.

Figure 5 shows the relationship between percentile ranks and z-scores for scores that are normally distributed. (Tests like this, which contain many items of intermediate difficulty, along with a few easy items and a few hard ones, produce scores distributed like this by design. See Appendix B.) This figure also illustrates that percentile ranks are clustered close together near the middle and spread out more at either end because many students' raw scores are near the middle of this distribution. So, the 5-point difference in percentile rank from the 10th to the 15th percentile or from the 90th to the 95th percentile is due to a larger raw score difference than the 5-point difference from the 50th to the 55th percentile.

Comparing students to the norm reference group. Once the characteristics of the norm reference group have been established, the performances of all other students can be put in this context.

When the test is given, the developers compare students' raw scores to the raw scores for the norm reference group. Each student's raw score is assigned the percentile rank of that score in the norm reference group. The student in our example, whose percentile rank is 84, had the same raw score as the student in the norm ref-

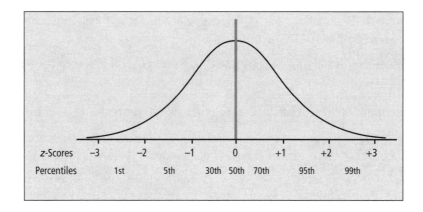

Fig. 5. Statistics for the norm reference group

erence group who scored at the 84th percentile. And, because the 84th percentile is one standard deviation above the 50th percentile score in the norm reference group, our student's *z*-score is +1.0.

Once they determine *z*-scores, the test developers can report a norm-referenced score for each student. They could report the *z*-score itself. More likely, they will report scores *derived* from the *z*-scores. For example, the Educational Testing Service reports scores for the SAT Reasoning Test in Mathematics that transform *z*-scores to scores with a mean value of 500 and a standard deviation of 100. The developers of our hypothetical Test A use the same approach to derive their scaled scores. So, our student's *z*-score of +1.0 is reported as a scaled score of 600.[5]

Our student's grade equivalent score of 9.5 is derived from an analysis of scores of a nationally representative random sample of ninth graders who were also given this eighth-grade test. Not surprisingly, these students will do somewhat better, as a group, than the eighth graders in the norm reference group. In our example, the raw score of the average ninth grader is the same as that of the eighth grader who scored at the 84th percentile (see fig. 6). These tests were given to the norm reference group—and to the ninth-grade sample—in the middle of the school year, so our student is assigned a grade equivalent score of 9.5.

It is easy to misinterpret grade equivalent scores. Someone might conclude that an eighth grader who earned a grade equivalent score of 9.5 on the Test A is capable of doing ninth-grade mathematics. However, this score means only that this student's performance was about what we would expect from the average ninth grader *who took this eighth-grade test* in the middle of the year.

—————

5. This is a linear transformation using the formula "scaled score = 500 + 100(*z*-score)."

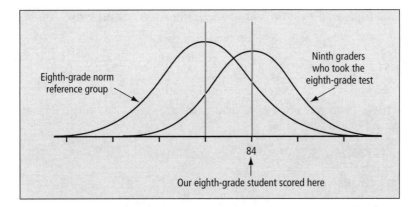

Fig. 6. Finding grade equivalent scores

In reality, grade equivalent scores are often only estimates. It is possible that no ninth graders actually took Test A. The test developers estimate scores like this one by interpolating (or extrapolating) the observed trend in increased performance across the grade levels of those who did take the test. In figure 7, our student's *z*-score of +1.0 is assigned a grade equivalent score using average scores from random samples of sixth, eighth, and tenth graders given this eighth-grade test.

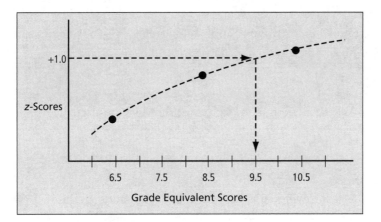

Fig. 7. A graph for estimating grade equivalent scores

So, what does our eighth-grade student know about eighth-grade mathematics? We have evidence that she scored higher than many students in the norm reference group, and we know she scored about the same as what we might expect from the average ninth grader taking this eighth-grade test. In other words, we know only comparative information. We do not know, from the evidence presented here, which of the topics on the test our student knows well and which topics gave her trouble.

Using Test B

How well will student scores from our hypothetical Test B answer the question, What do students know? For example, a student might obtain the following scores on this standards-based test:

- Scale Score: 575

- Performance Level: Developing

How are the scores on this test determined? What do they mean? What evidence do they provide about what students know?

Understanding the scale score. The developers of this test used a more recent approach to test design called Item Response Theory (IRT) (see Appendix C). They began by assuming that the mathematics knowledge to be measured by the test is *unidimensional.* In other words, students with little knowledge of the subject would appear at the low end of a single dimension, or scale, and students with a lot of knowledge would be at the high end of the same scale. In this instance, the scale runs from 200 to 1000, and our student's place on the scale is at 575 (see fig. 8).

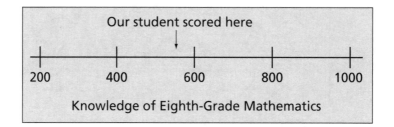

Fig. 8. Our student's place on the knowledge scale

How do the test developers determine that our student's knowledge is in this particular place on the scale? They begin by creating items that address the different content standards used by the district. For each item, they ask the following question: *"What is the chance that a student at a particular place on the scale will answer this item correctly?"*

Imagine giving one of these items to students possessing amounts of knowledge that are spread across the full length of the mathematics knowledge scale. Students at the low end of the scale will be less likely to answer the question correctly, whereas students at the high end will be more likely to get it right. The test developers are interested in the particular place on the knowledge scale where students will have a 50 percent chance of getting this item right. A graph of this information might look like the one in figure 9. This graph is called the *item characteristic curve* for this particular item. Every potential item on the test is analyzed this way.

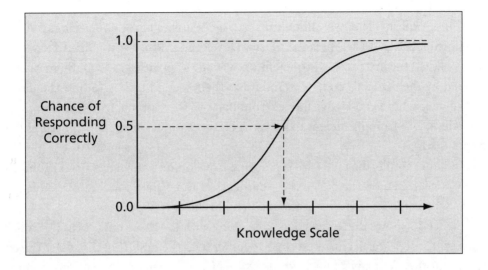

Fig. 9. A particular item's response data

Once this analysis is complete, the developers assemble a test. They select items that meet two conditions: they tap each of the district's content standards, and they span the knowledge scale from low to high.

Once the test is built, it is given to students. Each student will respond correctly to some items and incorrectly to others, producing a pattern of responses. The developers look at each student's pattern of responses and ask a second question: *"At what place on the scale would a student be most likely to produce this particular pattern of responses?"* To answer this question, developers have to reason backward. If they knew a student's place on the knowledge scale, then they could predict the most likely pattern of item responses. For example, a student near the middle of the scale would likely respond correctly to items low on the scale, incorrectly to items high on the scale, and with mixed results for items near the middle of the scale. However, all the developers have is the student's actual set of responses. So, their task is to find the place on the scale where a student is most likely to produce this particular set of responses. For our student, her most likely location on the scale of mathematics knowledge, according to her responses to the items on Test B, is 575. (For a more detailed description of this process, see Appendix D.)

Determining the performance level. Is a scale score of 575 a high score or a low score? What does this score mean for the school district? To answer this question, the test developers convene a group of experts to help them assign performance levels to different intervals along the knowledge scale.

These experts have two difficult tasks. The first is to agree about what the performance levels—in this instance, Basic, Developing, Proficient, and Advanced—mean. What, for instance, is Proficient knowledge of eighth-grade mathematics, as defined by the district's content standards? Their second task is to find the points on the scale where knowledge moves from Basic to Developing, from Developing to Proficient, and from Proficient to Advanced. These points are called *cut scores* (see Appendix F).

In our example, the cut score separating Developing knowledge from Proficient knowledge, based on the collective judgments of the expert panel, is 576. Our student's score of 575 places her at the high end of the Developing level.

Figure 10 shows the knowledge scale along with the three cut scores for Test B. These cut scores are all clustered close together near the middle of the scale. The cut scores for the company's fourth-grade test will also be clustered, but lower on this common mathematics knowledge scale. Similarly, the cut scores for the twelfth-grade test will cluster toward the high end of the scale. Scale scores for all students are measurements along the same scale; cut scores define performance levels for students at particular grade levels.

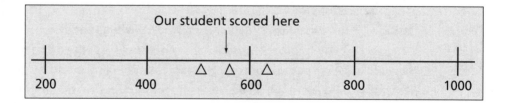

Fig. 10. Cut scores for Test B

How much mathematics does our student know? The evidence from the scale score and performance level suggests that our student has a moderate amount of mathematics knowledge and that in the collective judgment of experts, this knowledge is at the high end of Developing, but not quite Proficient, for eighth-grade mathematics students. The complex procedures used to estimate our student's scale score and the judgments that led to the setting of cut scores add uncertainty to any conclusions drawn about our student's knowledge of eighth-grade mathematics. As we turn to the next proposed use of test evidence, we discuss in more detail the sources—and the consequences for students—of this uncertainty.

Proposed Use 2: What Ninth-Grade Class?

Our school district, like most across the country, has been placing students in one of three ninth-grade mathematics courses—the typical ninth-grade course or an honors course, both of which earn high school mathematics credit toward graduation, or a remedial course, which does not—using some combination of the following: middle school courses taken, students' grades in those courses, teachers' recommendations, and parents' requests. The committee was asked to consider how standardized test evidence might be included in these decisions and which of the two tests would be best for this purpose.

This use of test evidence raises the stakes for the district's students. Unlike the reporting of what students know, the committee was now considering a use of test data that would likely have important consequences for the opportunities students have in their high school mathematics programs. Acknowledging that at this point they were venturing into more challenging terrain, the committee looked at each of the tests in turn.

Could Test A be used?

Students might be placed in their ninth-grade courses using the scores on Test A and the following criteria:

- A student who scores at grade level or above (that is, a grade equivalent score of 8.5 or higher on this test, which was given in the middle of eighth grade, a percentile rank of 50 or higher, or a scaled score of 500 or higher) would be placed in high school mathematics.

- Honors placement would be reserved for those students who score at or above the 90th percentile (scaled score at or above 640; grade equivalent score of at least 10.5).

- All other students would be placed in the remedial course.

Do these criteria make sense? Are they valid uses of evidence from Test A? To what extent do scores on this test accurately assess students' need for remedial work, their readiness for high school mathematics, or their readiness for the challenges of the honors program?

Test content. Test A contains items spread across the broad, common-denominator list of topics the test company has established for eighth-grade mathematics. The district's eighth-grade mathematics curriculum is but a subset of this broad list of topics. And the set of items on this test is just a sample of all possible items that tap this content. So this or any domain-sampled test is unlikely to be very well aligned with the district's stated curriculum.

In addition, this use of test data might influence the district's taught curriculum itself. Because of the higher stakes for students, middle schools are likely to make curriculum and instruction choices that emphasize content that appears on the test and de-emphasize content that does not. This constraining effect might further undermine the alignment between the curriculum and the state's standards.

Norm-referenced scoring. All the scores reported for our student give evidence of how she performed compared to the students in the national norm reference group. Our student performed better on this test than 84 percent of the students in that group, but did she perform well or poorly? Is she prepared for high school mathematics or for the rigors of the honors program? Does she need remedial work, and if so, in what areas? There are, in this set of relative scores, no answers to these questions.

Error. The scores on this test are measurements, and they thus contain measurement error. Our student's observed scores are only estimates of her true score, what we might find if it were possible to measure without any error at all.

Of course, it is impossible to eliminate measurement error. So, if it were possible to give this test to our student over and over, we would—just as we would if we repeatedly measured her height with a meterstick—obtain a range of measurements. Some scores would be too high; others, too low. Most would be close to the true value; a few will be relatively far off. Many such measurements would be approximately normally distributed around the true score, and the standard deviation of this collection of measurements—known as the standard error of measurement—would give some idea of how far from our student's true score we might expect her actual test score to be (see Appendix A).

Students who take Test A receive scaled scores between 200 and 800. The standard error of measurement for this test, as it is for the well-known SAT Reasoning Test in Mathematics, is 30 points. Our student's score of 600 is actually only an estimate of her true score. We can be 95 percent certain that her true score lies somewhere between 540 and 660 (two standard errors on either side of the observed score). Given this lack of precision, in which ninth-grade course should she be placed?

Our student's scores are also compromised by sampling error. The national norm reference group was chosen by the testing company to be nationally representative. That is, they were meant to approximate a cross section of all the country's eighth graders. If our committee's school district has a student population similar to the national population, then our student's scores will approximate her relative standing in this district. But what if the district's eighth graders are not like all the country's eighth graders? Our student's 84th percentile rank might be a relatively low score, for example, if there happen to be many high scorers in this district (as is often true in districts in affluent communities).

Given the lack of alignment of its domain-sampled content, with relative scores that are only approximate and say little about what students actually know, the evidence offered by this test seems inadequate for the high-stakes use of placing students in their ninth-grade mathematics courses.

Could Test B be used?

This test, designed to address the state's mathematics standards, seems at first glance to be better suited for placing eighth graders in their ninth-grade classes. The committee might be asked to consider the following placement policy:

- Students who score Proficient or above would be placed in high school mathematics.

- Honors placement would be reserved for those students who score Advanced.

- All other students, those who score Basic or Developing, would be placed in the remedial course.

Can these criteria be applied in a meaningful and fair way? Given the stakes for students, do these policies make sense?

Test content and error. This test was built using standards-based sampling, in an attempt to align the test with the district's mathematics standards. But even with standards-based sampling only a small set of items can be chosen to address each of the standards, so this alignment is only approximate. Because of sampling error in the items chosen and because of errors in measurement, our student's scale score is really only an estimate of her actual place on the knowledge scale.

This is not the only concern about this high-stakes use of the test data. The middle schools of the district have adopted curriculum materials that, in their judgment, address adequately each of the content strands outlined in their standards. But this alignment is not perfect. So the taught curriculum is only approximately aligned with the standards. This means that there is a good deal of uncertainty about

37

the alignment of this test with students' actual opportunities to learn. And as with Test A, this proposed use of the test will likely have the effect of narrowing curriculum and instruction choices made by teachers, further muddying the picture.

More error. Figure 11 shows a dot plot of students' scale scores on Test B. The vertical lines show the three cut scores. In this figure, we have zoomed in on our student's scale score, which is just below the cut score for Proficient.

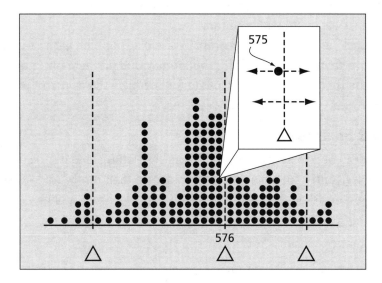

Fig. 11. Students' scale scores and cut scores on Test B

Both her scale score of 575, and the cut score of 576, are only approximations. If we include these errors, it is not clear if our student's actual place on the scale is above or below the cut score. Is her score Proficient or Developing? For students whose scale scores are close to the cut scores, this question cannot be answered with certainty.

The assumption of unidimensionality. Can students be placed along a single scale according to their knowledge of eighth-grade mathematics? The designers of Test B make this assumption. We noted in our discussion of difficulty that there are many dimensions of mathematical proficiency. One widely used distinction is between conceptual knowledge and procedural knowledge. An eighth grader might, for example, know a procedure for solving a proportion like

$$\frac{5}{12} = \frac{x}{30}$$

without knowing where that procedure came from or why it works. Another eighth grader might also know *when* two situations are directly proportional and *why* an equation like this one appropriately represents this relationship. This conceptual knowledge is another, somewhat different aspect of the knowledge of ratios and proportions. Another, more nuanced model (Kilpatrick, Swafford, and Findell 2001) describes mathematical proficiency as consisting of five intertwined threads: conceptual understanding, procedural fluency, strategic competence, adaptive reasoning, and productive disposition. Whatever the view of the complex construct of mathematical knowledge, the designers of Test B collapse it all into one dimension and then rank students from low to high along this dimension. What are the contributions of each of these dimensions to students' scale scores? The single scale score gives no answers to this question.

Proposed Use 3:
How Good Are the Schools' Mathematics Programs?

The committee knows that to answer this question, the district will be making two types of comparisons: one school to another school in a particular year, and each school's results from year to year. Norm-referenced data from Test A might be used for these comparisons. The district could compute average scores for each of the middle schools and for the district. These school averages could be compared to each other and tracked over time, and the district's average could be compared to the average score of the norm reference group.

Of course, scores from Test B could be used in much the same way. Each school's average scale score could be computed, and the number of students in each school at each of the four achievement levels could be tallied. Armed with these summaries, the district could compare schools to one another or track a school's performance from year to year.

Test B data and these statistical summaries could also be used to set performance standards for schools. The district could set the goal that each school will have all (or some high proportion of) its eighth graders at or above Proficient by some future date. It could rate the schools according to their actual proportion of Proficient and Advanced students each year between now and then, and it could set requirements for schools to show a certain amount of improvement in these proportions each year.

The validity of each of these school comparisons is limited by the accumulation of errors contributed by each individual student's score, by inadequate attention to the distribution of scores in each school, and by the effects of having nonrandom samples of students in each school.

Aggregated error

We have already described the errors that are an unavoidable part of students' individual scores on these tests. By aggregating the scores of the students in a school, such as by finding the mean of all students' scale scores, the district will be aggregating these errors as well. Each school's mean score will also have error, so—just as with the comparison between two students' individual scores—any comparison between two schools' mean scores will have to take into account this error. (See Appendix G.)

The distribution of scores

Whenever data are summarized statistically, information is lost. If the district uses mean scale scores to compare schools without considering the distribution of scores at each school, it runs the risk of making the mistake illustrated by figure 12. In this example, School A has a higher mean score than School B. However, because of the skewed distributions, School B has more high-scoring students than School A. Which school performed better?

The distribution of scores matters even if schools are compared using the percent of students at each performance level. Imagine, for example, compar-

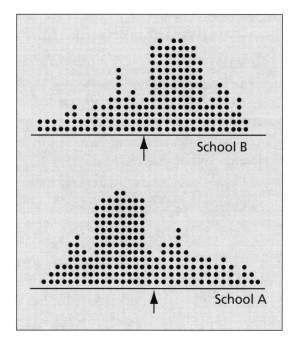

Fig. 12. Two schools' means and distributions

ing a school's performance one year with its performance the next year using the percent of students who score Proficient or better each year on Test B. If this percent does not change appreciably from one year to the next, one might conclude that the school's performance had not improved. But this ignores the possibility that the school had focused its instructional efforts on improving the performances of those students who scored lowest the first year, and although those students performed much better the next year, none of them reached the Proficient level. Without looking at the distribution of scores, the district would miss these improvements.

Faced with this possibility, schools might choose instead to focus their instructional efforts primarily on those students who have already scored close to the Proficient cut score. In this way, improvements are more likely to improve the school's standing. However, this decision might divert scarce instructional resources from the most needy students.

Nonrandom samples

If we were interested in whether young voters differ from older voters on a particular political issue, we might select manageable samples from each group, ask them their opinions, and then use their responses to make inferences about the larger groups. The challenge is to determine whether any observed differences between the two samples are due to who was chosen, or if they represent real differences between the two larger groups. Choosing random samples makes this job easier; any sampling errors introduced by not asking all young voters and all seniors are small and predictable.

When comparing the standardized test scores of the eighth graders at School A with those of School B, the district's leaders want to know which school performed better. They hope to draw conclusions about which school did a better job; did School A's eighth-grade mathematics program better educate students than School B's program? To make this inference, they must treat the students at each school as random samples of the larger group of eighth graders who could have attended these schools during this time. However, *the students who attend School A and School B are not randomly selected.* For example, many students attend schools close to home, and the demographics and economics of neighborhoods can vary widely. The consequence of nonrandom samples is that it is difficult to attribute test score differences to differences in the educational programs of the schools. We offer two examples of the interpretation problems created by the nonrandom samples of students in schools.

Comparing schools. The graph in figure 13 compares two sets of data from a school district. For each school, the percent of students who qualify for free or reduced lunch is plotted along the horizontal axis, and the percent of students who scored Proficient or Advanced on the state mathematics test is plotted along the vertical axis.

41

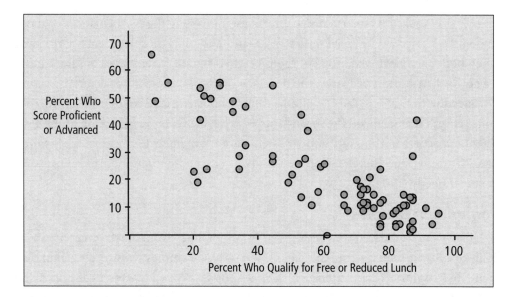

Fig. 13. The relationship between aggregate test scores and socioeconomic status[6]

Schools in which a high percentage of students qualify for free or reduced lunch (which requires a sufficiently low family income) tend to have a lower percentage of students doing well on the state test. These are neighborhood schools, so the range of family incomes of the district's students is not distributed randomly across the schools. If the test performance of a school on the left side of this plot were compared to that of a school on the right, it would be difficult to attribute the likely numerical difference to differences in the mathematics teaching and learning experiences offered by the two schools. Comparisons between schools that do not take into account this very strong association (in this instance the correlation is close to −0.8) run the risk of concluding, unjustifiably, that the schools in the poorest neighborhoods are doing the worst jobs.

School performance over time. A recent study examined the performance over time of 734 elementary schools on that state's fourth-grade reading test. Overall, the state's schools showed, on average, a solid 4.7 percent improvement in their scores from 1997 to 2000. However, only 4.9 percent of the schools improved by 1 percent or more for each of the three comparison periods of 1997–1998, 1998–1999, and 1999–2000 (Linn, Baker, and Betebenner 2002). The state seemed to be making real

---

6. These data were collected by the author from 81 elementary schools in a large, urban school district.

improvement during this time period, but few of the individual schools showed "adequate yearly progress" of 1 percent improvement per year if their performances are tracked from year to year. Why?

In this instance, nonrandom samples combine with aggregated error to make conclusions difficult to draw. The students in a school change from one year to the next, as older students leave, younger students enter, and students transfer. And none of these samples of students is randomly selected. So, what larger group of students do they represent? In addition, one-time changes in the school from one year to the next (such as faculty turnover) and policy changes that affect the number of students at a school who take the test (such as the exclusion of special education students) will be sources of test score differences that have little to do with the quality of a school's mathematics program.

As a result of this sampling error and the measurement error discussed earlier, a school's aggregate score might appear to drop over time because of an overestimate one year followed by an underestimate the next. This might obscure a true gain in performance. With all the uncertainty surrounding a school's yearly scores, it is unlikely that the school could meet ambitious performance goals year after year, even if its instructional program is improving.

Implications

Well-intentioned educators and policymakers from across the political spectrum share the goal of improving students' learning of mathematics in school. Standardized tests play central—and increasingly controversial—roles in federal, state, and local programs designed to meet this goal. We have used the example of a school district evaluating evidence from two types of standardized tests to illustrate some of the implications of this role for large-scale assessments. Our school district is left with the inescapable conclusion that neither of the two tests will, alone, answer conclusively its questions about its students' knowledge of mathematics, about the courses in which students should be placed, or about the quality of instruction provided by its schools. Their experience suggests that educators and policymakers who wish to use evidence from standardized tests seek clear answers to the following important questions (AERA, APA , and NCME 1999):

- What does the test claim to measure?

- How well does the test measure what it claims to measure?

- For what uses has the test been validated?

• What are the limitations of evidence provided by the test?

All stakeholders in the mathematics education of children have the obligation to use data from large-scale assessments responsibly. We have presented some of the facts of standardized tests. We hope that, armed with these facts, readers will be better able to analyze the quality of evidence furnished by these tests, to argue for valid uses of this evidence, and to argue persuasively against abuses of test data that undermine schools' ability to support the development of real mathematical power for all children.

REFERENCES

American Educational Research Association, American Psychological Association, and National Council on Measurement in Education (AERA, APA, and NCME). *Standards for Educational and Psychological Testing.* Washington, D.C.: AERA, 1999.

Bass, Kristin M., and Robert Glaser. "Developing Assessments to Inform Teaching and Learning." CSE Report 628. Los Angeles: National Center for Research on Evaluation, Standards, and Student Testing (CRESST), 2004.

Bracey, Gerald. *Thinking about Tests and Testing: A Short Primer in Assessment Literacy.* Washington, D.C.: American Youth Policy Forum, 2000.

Bush, William S., and Anja S. Greer, eds. *Mathematics Assessment: A Practical Handbook for Grades 9–12.* Reston, Va.: National Council of Teachers of Mathematics, 1999.

Kilpatrick, Jeremy, Jane Swafford, and Bradford Findell. *Adding It Up: Helping Children Learn Mathematics.* Washington, D.C.: National Academy Press, 2001.

Linn, Robert L., Eva L. Baker, and Damian W. Betebenner. "Accountability Systems: Implications of Requirements of the No Child Left Behind Act of 2001." CSE Technical Report 567, June 2002. Available at www.cse.ucla.edu.

National Council of Teachers of Mathematics (NCTM). *Assessment Standards for School Mathematics.* Reston, Va.: NCTM, 1995.

————. *Principles and Standards for School Mathematics.* Reston, Va.: NCTM, 2000.

National Research Council. *Knowing What Students Know: The Science and Design of Educational Assessment.* Washington, D.C.: National Academy Press, 2001.

Shepard, Lorrie A. "The Role of Assessment in a Learning Culture." *Educational Researcher* 29 (October 2000): 4–14.

Wiggins, Grant. *Educative Assessment: Designing Assessments to Inform and Improve Student Performance.* San Francisco: Jossey-Bass, 1998.

ADDITIONAL READING

Books

Crocker, Linda, and James Algina. *Introduction to Classical and Modern Test Theory.* Orlando, Fla.: Holt, Rinehart & Winston, 1986.

Gould, Stephen Jay. *The Mismeasure of Man.* New York: W. W. Norton & Co., 1981.

National Research Council. *High Stakes: Testing for Tracking, Promotion, and Graduation.* Washington, D.C.: National Academy Press, 1999. Available at www.nap.edu/catalog/6336.html.

————. *Knowing What Students Know: The Science and Design of Educational Assessment.* Washington, D.C.: National Academy Press, 2001. Available at www.nap.edu/catalog/10019.html.

Organizations

National Board on Educational Testing and Public Policy (www.bc.edu/research/nbetpp). Papers produced by this organization, available on its Web site, include the following:

Horn, Catherine, Miguel Ramos, Irwin Blumer, and George Madaus. "Cut Scores: Results May Vary." Monographs Series, Vol. 1, No. 1, April 2000.

Shore, Arnold, Joseph Pedulla, and Marguerite Clarke. "The Building Blocks of State Testing Programs." Statements Series, Vol. 2, No. 4, August 2001.

National Center for Research on Evaluation, Standards, and Student Testing (www.cse.ucla.edu). Papers produced by this organization, available on its Web site, include the following:

Misleavy, Robert J., Mark R. Wilson, Kadriye Ercikan, and Naomi Chudowsky. "Psychometric Principles in Student Assessment." CSE Technical Report 583, December 2002.

Appendix A:
Some Basics of Classical Test Theory

Test A was designed using the principles of Classical Test Theory, which has guided the design of tests since early in the twentieth century. Here is Classical Test Theory in a nutshell: a student's score on a test, her *observed score*, is an estimate of that student's *true score*, subject to some random *error*. Written as an equation,

$$\text{observed score} = \text{true score} + \text{error}.$$

For any student, therefore, repeated administrations of the test would produce a set of observed scores that differ from one another because of the measurement errors that are part of each score. These errors are random and do not depend in any way on the student's true score, so the observed scores are as likely to overestimate the student's true score as they are to underestimate it. (In other words, they are unbiased estimates.) The set of observed scores will be normally distributed, and the student's true score is defined as the mean of this distribution.[7] The standard deviation of this distribution of observed scores is called the *standard error of measurement* (see fig. A-1).

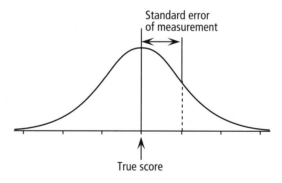

Fig. A-1. The hypothetical distribution of observed scores around a student's true score

Of course, it is impossible to give a test over and over again to the same student. In reality, a student will take a test only once, and the score on that test, the observed

---

7. "True score" is a statistical concept. This definition is sufficient for our purposes, but it sidesteps the issue of whether true scores are real characteristics of test takers. The history of Classical Test Theory is intertwined with the century-long history of measurement of innate intelligence. Much of this work ascribed differences in average scores on intelligence tests among groups to real differences in innate intelligence among those groups.

score, will be the only information we have to estimate the student's true score. (In this way, giving a test is just like conducting a survey.) To estimate a student's true score from just one observed score, we would need to know the relationship between observed scores and the true score. That relationship is called the *reliability* of the test.

Conceptually, the reliability of a test is a comparison of the true scores of a group of students to their observed scores. Imagine that a group of students is given a test. The collection of true scores for these students (if we could collect them) would have a certain amount of variability because, after all, they are different students. The observed scores of these students will also be variable, but that variability will be greater because each observed score also contains some error. The *reliability coefficient*, called ρ (the Greek letter rho), is found by comparing the variability in true scores to the variability in observed scores:

$$\rho = \frac{\text{variability in true scores}}{\text{variability in observed scores}}$$

This comparison will always have a value less than +1. (The value would be equal to +1 if there were no measurement error and the two sets of scores were equally variable. But there's always measurement error.) Small measurement errors will produce observed scores distributed not much more widely than true scores, so the value of ρ will be closer to +1. Large measurement errors will increase the variability of observed scores relative to true scores, and the value of ρ will be closer to 0.

Therefore, a highly reliable test is one with small measurement errors and observed scores that are better estimates of the student's true score. In other words, the confidence interval around a student's observed score will be smaller. The reliability of a test is a measure of the *consistency* of students' performances over repeated administrations of the test. Alternatively, it is a measure of the *accuracy* or *precision* of the measurements the test is designed to make.

In reality, we cannot collect the true scores needed to make the comparison described above. In practice, the reliability coefficient is estimated using actual test data. Several methods have been developed for this, and each of them relies on the relationship between reliability and correlation. A highly reliable test will have small measurement errors. Therefore, the scores of repeated administrations of the test will not differ much; that is, they will be highly correlated. We'll describe two methods that make use of this connection.

Test-retest. One way to estimate the reliability of a test is to give the test to a group of students, and then some time later give it again to the same students under the same conditions. If you wait long enough so that students do not remember the test questions, but not so long that students' knowledge has changed, the scores on the two tests will vary only because of measurement error. The correlation between these two sets of scores will be an estimate of the test's reliability.

Split-half. The test-retest method described above requires that the test be given twice. The split-half method requires only one test administration. If the test can be divided into two subtests, each with half the items and as similar to each other as possible (that is, as nearly parallel as possible), then students' performances on one half of the test can be compared to their performances on the other half. The correlation between the two will be an estimate of the test's reliability. This method correlates scores on two subtests that are shorter than the original test. Shorter tests are less reliable than longer tests, just as surveys using smaller samples have more error than those that use larger ones. Therefore, this method tends to underestimate the reliability of a test. However, several techniques are available to estimate the reliability of the full-length test.[8]

To summarize, when a student takes a test, her score on that test—her observed score—is an estimate of her true score. The accuracy of that estimate depends on the relative size of the errors of measurement for the test and is expressed as the reliability of the test.

---

8. A statistic called Cronbach's α provides a lower bound on the estimate of the reliability of a full test derived from correlations among subtests.

Appendix B:
Building and Testing Test Items

The designers of Test A begin the process of developing test items by deciding on the range of item formats. In this example, they decide to use both *selected-response* items and *constructed-response* items. For the selected-response items, they decide to write multiple-choice questions, items with a question (or prompt) followed by a list of possible answers (or distractors). For constructed-response items, they write (1) some questions that require the students only to fill in an answer and (2) other questions that ask for both an answer and an explanation. Finally, they develop an answer key. This key includes correct choices for the multiple-choice items and, for each of the constructed-response items, their predictions for the range of possible student responses. For items that require an answer and an explanation, they design a scoring guide, or rubric.

The pool of potential items is then posed to a random sample of eighth graders. Their responses are analyzed to determine how the items "function." First, the developers calculate the proportion of students in the sample who answered each item correctly. This proportion, a decimal between 0.0 and 1.0, determines the *item difficulty, p*.[9] For example, an item with $p = 0.8$ has low difficulty, because 80 percent of the sample students answered it correctly.

Second, the test developers calculate the relationship (that is, the correlation) between students' performance on each item and their performance on the whole test. Their goal here is to identify items that high-scoring students are likely to answer correctly and that low-scoring students are likely to answer incorrectly. These items are said to *discriminate*, or differentiate, between students who know the content being tested and those who do not.

Item difficulty and item discrimination are related ideas. Items that are too easy or too hard do not discriminate well. For example, easy items are items that a high proportion of students answered correctly, including those who scored lower on the overall test. The relationship between performance on this item and performance on the test will be low. Items of intermediate difficulty ($p \approx 0.5$) tend to discriminate best.

However, even items of intermediate difficulty may discriminate poorly. If the item is ambiguously written, students all across the knowledge spectrum might an-

---

9. Another index of item difficulty, Δ (delta), is sometimes calculated. This index, a transformation of the difficulty index p onto a wider numerical scale, is used in studies of item bias.

swer correctly or incorrectly for reasons having little to do with what they know, and the relationship between their responses on this item and their responses on the entire test will be low. The ideal items for Test A, whose purpose is to compare a student's performance to that of others, have intermediate difficulty and high discrimination.

We note here that the estimates of the true scores of a group of students will be affected by the characteristics of the test they are given. For example, a very difficult test is likely to produce a lower estimate of the true score. In addition, the characteristics of the test depend on the sample of students used to derive them. A sample containing many similarly strong students will produce item difficulty and discrimination indexes lower than if the same items were tested on a more heterogeneous group of students. Therefore, it was important for the designers of Test A to test their test on representative samples of U.S. eighth graders.

The analysis of items includes a check for one additional property. Do different groups of students perform differently on specific items? Do the responses of male students differ from those of female students in some systematic way? Do students with limited proficiency in English perform worse than other students? If so, this difference in performance may be due to something other than the students' knowledge of eighth-grade mathematics. Including items like these on the test may bias the estimates of these students' true scores by introducing a source of systematic error. This check for *differential item functioning* (known as DIF) is one essential step in the creation of a fair test.

Appendix C:
Item Response Theory

Test B was designed using the principles of a modern approach to test development known as Item Response Theory (IRT). The test developers begin by focusing on individual items instead of on the test as a whole. Once items with particular characteristics have been developed, whole tests are constructed from them.

The principal idea underlying IRT is that for any test item, the chance that a student will respond to that item correctly will depend on the amount of some *latent trait* possessed by that student. In our example, the latent trait of interest is the knowledge of eighth-grade mathematics. Figure C-1 shows the latent trait, θ, as a one-dimensional scale, with two students at different positions on that scale. Student *a* will be less likely to answer a given item correctly than Student *b*.[10]

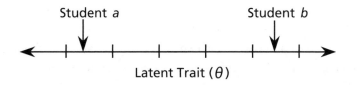

Fig. C-1. A unidimensional latent trait scale

The first task for test developers is to determine, for every item in their pool of items, the actual relationship between a student's position on the latent trait scale and the probability that she will answer the item correctly. This specific relationship is portrayed in a graph like the one in figure C-2, called an *item characteristic curve.*

For a student at or below position *a* on the knowledge scale, the chance of a correct response to this item is very low, whereas a student at or above position *b* is very likely to respond correctly. Position *c* on the scale marks the point at which a student will have a 50 percent chance of responding to the item correctly.

The item with this curve will not discriminate very well among students above position *b* on the scale. All these students are very likely to respond the same way to

---

10. As with the true scores of Classical Test Theory, this assumption about a student's position on the latent trait scale is a statistical one. However, just as before, we note that it does not necessarily follow that students (or groups of students) with different θ values possess different amounts of innate ability.

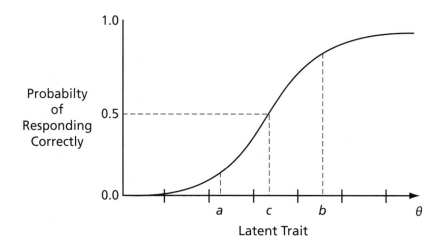

Fig. C-2. Item characteristic curve for a given item

the item. For the same reason, the item will discriminate poorly among students below position *a* on the scale. However, this item is sensitive to small differences among students located between scale values *a* and *b*. In this interval, the curve is steep; a small increase in the value of θ will increase the chance that the student will respond to the item correctly.

The item characteristic curve for each item is found by fitting a mathematical equation to student response data.[11] Different items will have item characteristic curves with different features. For more difficult items, the amount of knowledge needed to have a 50 percent chance of getting the item right will be higher on the scale. For items that discriminate more sensitively, their item characteristic curves will be steeper (see fig. C-3).

The test developers construct their test using items that are sensitive to students at different points on the knowledge scale. Figure C-4 shows four items whose item characteristic curves place them at different points on the knowledge scale. Student *a* is likely to respond to each of the four items incorrectly; Student *b* is likely to get all of them correct; Student *c* is most likely to answer (1) and (2) correctly and (3) and (4) incorrectly.

---

11. This process, which uses data from many test takers and entails many iterative steps, is both complicated and computationally intense. The basic S-shaped mathematical model is called a "logistic" function, and the values of several coefficients (or parameters) determine the position and shape of the graph. Using a computer, test developers make initial guesses for the values of these parameters and of students' θ values and then go through a guess-and-check procedure to find the most likely parameter values.

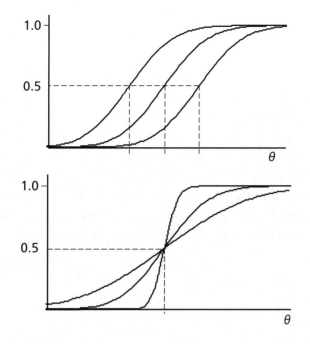

Fig. C-3. Item characteristic curves for three items with the same levels of discrimination but different levels of difficulty (top) and with the same difficulty but different levels of discrimination (bottom)

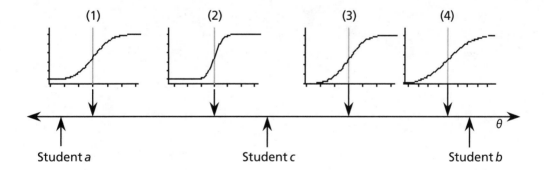

Fig. C-4. Item characteristic curves for four items along the knowledge scale

When we outlined the principles of Classical Test Theory, we noted that the characteristics of students who take a test (such as their knowledge of eighth-grade mathematics) and the characteristics of the test itself (item difficulty and discrimination indexes, for example) are inseparable. Students who take a difficult test will seem to have lower levels of achievement than if they had taken an easier test, and a stronger sample of students will make items on a test seem easier (see Appendix B).

IRT was developed to address these consequences of the Classical Test Theory approach. IRT is based on two assumptions. The first is that the curve-fitting process used to find the item characteristic curve for a given item produces a relationship that *does not depend on the test takers used to find it.* The chance that a student will answer a question correctly depends only on her place on the knowledge scale. So, if a student does answer a question correctly, one can use the item characteristic curve to get some information about the student's θ value. The second assertion of IRT is that a student's performance on a test—the estimate of the student's place on the latent trait scale derived from her responses to the items on the test—does not depend on the specific items used. (We elaborate on this in Appendix D.)

Appendix D:
Finding a Scale Score on Test B

Each of the items on Test B is sensitive to a specific place on the knowledge scale, and a test is assembled so that items span that scale. Imagine that Test B consists of ten items spread across the scale as shown in figure D-1.

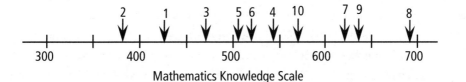

Fig. D-1. Scale positions of the ten items on Test B

When a student takes this test, her answer to each question furnishes some information about her knowledge of eighth-grade mathematics and, therefore, about her place on the scale. For example, imagine she answers item 7 correctly. This is a very unlikely response if her knowledge is at 400 on this scale, moderately likely if her scale value is 625, and highly likely if her scale value is 750. The job of the test developer is to use the information provided by the student's responses to each of the test items to find the student's location on the scale.

The table in figure D-2 shows the responses of two students to the full set of ten items posed on Test B. A correct response is coded 1, and an incorrect response is coded 0.

	2	1	3	5	6	4	10	7	9	8
Student *a*	1	1	0	1	1	1	1	0	1	0
Student *b*	1	0	0	1	0	1	0	0	0	0

Fig. D-2. Test B response patterns for two students

In this table, the items are listed in order of their difficulty; that is, their position on the scale. These response patterns indicate that Student *a*, who has answered more—and more difficult—items correctly, is likely to have knowledge of eighth-grade mathematics that would place her higher on the scale than Student *b*. What specific scale values are the *most likely ones* to produce the response patterns for these students?

Here is how the process would work for Student *a*. We would start by assuming a low scale value for Student *a*. Then, we would use the test's item characteristic curves to find the probabilities that she would answer each of the items the way she did. Finally, we would multiply these probabilities to find the probability that this assumed position on the scale would produce this specific set of responses.[12] For example, if we assume Student *a*'s knowledge of eighth-grade mathematics would place her at a scale value of 300, it is unlikely she would answer any questions correctly. The chance that she would present seven correct answers will be low, and the product of the probabilities will be low as well. Thus, the chance that she is at scale value 300 is low.

Next, we would increase the assumed scale value for Student *a* by small amounts and repeat this process. When we get to an assumed scale value of 550, the chance of responding correctly to questions 2, 1, 3, 5, and 6 would be high, the chance of responding correctly to questions 4 and 10 would be moderate, and the chance of answering incorrectly to questions 7, 9, and 8 would also be high. Her actual responses matched this pattern reasonably well; for this assumed scale value, the probability of her specific response pattern will be relatively high. When we assume her scale value is 800, we would expect her to answer all ten questions correctly, so the low probabilities associated with her three incorrect answers would lower the overall probability of getting this set of responses.

Once we have done this for values across the scale, we would search the resulting list of probabilities for the highest value, the *maximum-likelihood estimation* of student *a*'s scale score. If we were to graph these results, it might look like the one in figure D-3. The high point of this graph marks the maximum-likelihood estimate of student *a*'s scale score.

A student's scale score—only an estimate of her place on the knowledge scale because the probabilities on which it is based are only estimates—depends only on the characteristics of each of the items on the test and the student's responses to those items. Another student could be placed on the same scale even if she an-

---

12. Individual item probabilities are multiplied together because a student's responses to the different items on a test are assumed to be *independent*, that is, her answer to one question does not affect her answer to any other question.

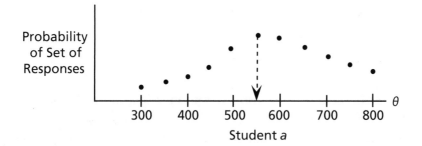

Fig. D-3. The maximum-likelihood estimate of Student a's scale score

swered different items, as long as the item characteristics are known. Therefore, test scaling and equating procedures such as those used for Test A (see Appendix E) are not needed here for IRT-based tests.[13]

---

13. This property of IRT-based tests permits a new kind of testing program called *computerized adaptive testing*. During an adaptive testing session, a student responds to initial questions posed by a computer. Subsequent questions are chosen by the computer on the basis of these initial responses. For example, correct answers will generate more difficult questions. In this way, a student will not be required to respond to questions well above or below her level of competence, and a much shorter, more targeted test is possible.

Appendix E: Test Score Equating

Test score equating establishes a relationship among scores on different tests. There are two reasons for equating scores. First, many test developers construct several alternative versions of a test. These alternative forms might have some items in common; they might have the same items appearing in a different order; they might have no items in common at all. So, in any test administration, different students might be taking somewhat different, or completely different, tests. In addition, many different tests are designed to measure the same thing (such as knowledge of eighth-grade mathematics). *Horizontal equating* of test scores converts a score on one test to the equivalent score on another test designed to measure the same construct (in our example, eighth graders who take different forms of Test A).

The second reason for equating scores is illustrated by the following example. Imagine the developers of Test A, an eighth-grade test, have also developed sixth-grade and tenth-grade mathematics tests as part of their "tests of mathematics knowledge" series. A district might decide that the tenth-grade test is a more appropriate test for eighth graders who are in its accelerated courses. However, the district also wants an eighth-grade mathematics score for every eighth-grade student. *Vertical equating* will establish a relationship between an eighth grader's score on the tenth-grade test and an equivalent score if that student had taken the eighth-grade test.

Test developers equate test scores by conducting equating studies. In one common type of study, which can be conducted as part of regular test administration, the developers will add a common set of items, called *anchor items*, to each of the alternative forms of the test. Responses of students in the two groups to these common items are used to establish the relationship needed to convert scores on one test to scores on the other.

Here are two real examples of test equating. First, each administration of the SAT includes a set of anchor items that are not counted in the scoring of the test but are answered by all test takers. Their responses are used to equate performances on the many alternative forms of the test. Second, students who take the Advanced Placement Calculus AB and Calculus BC tests answer a common subset of questions. For students who take the Calculus BC test, the Educational Testing Service also reports a "Calculus AB subscore." This is a prediction, based on the student's performance on the subset of AB items that appeared on the BC test, of what the student's score would have been if she had taken the full Calculus AB test.

Appendix F: Setting Cut Scores

Once each student is assigned a scale score on Test B, the test developers plan to categorize the performance of each student using one of four labels: Advanced, Proficient, Developing, or Basic. To accomplish this, the developers must decide what is a Proficient performance, for example, and what scale value will separate Proficient performance from performance that is merely Developing. The scale score values that separate one category of performance from another are called *cut scores*.[14]

To accomplish this task, the developers would convene a group of experts, often including both experienced eighth-grade mathematics teachers and university mathematics educators. The first part of this group's deliberations would be given over to defining the four performance levels. The group would discuss at length the characteristics of a student whom they would consider "proficient" at eighth-grade mathematics, and what characteristics distinguish the other levels of performance.

The experts would then be led through one of several different procedures for setting cut scores. In one procedure, they would review each of the items on Test B. For each item, they would be asked to use their best judgment to estimate the probability that a proficient student would answer that item correctly. Each of the experts would assign a high value to those items that, in her judgment, were "easy" for a proficient student, and a low p value to those items she thinks a proficient student would find "hard." The sum of her p values would be her estimate of the cut score.

The developers would set the cut score for Proficient using the average value of the totals provided by each of the experts.[15] They would then follow the same procedure to set the cut scores for Developing and Advanced.

In another cut-score-setting procedure, the developers would give each of the experts a list of the items on the test in order of their position on the latent trait scale. (This is called an item map.) They would ask each expert to review the items in this order and mark the first item they encounter that a Basic student would find difficult. This "bookmark"[16] will point to a place on the knowledge scale. The panelists' average place on the scale would be the cut score for Developing. Similarly, the

---

14. Cut scores are also used on some tests to classify examinees into two groups: "qualified" or "unqualified." For example, many states now use standardized tests as one criterion for obtaining a high school diploma. On each of these tests, a single cut score must be met or exceeded to meet the criterion.

15. This method of setting cut scores is referred to as the Angoff method.

16. The bookmarking procedure for setting cut scores was developed by the test publisher CTB/McGraw-Hill.

cut score for Proficient would combine experts' judgments of the place in the item map where Developing students would have difficulty answering items correctly.

An important feature of the second method described here is that it connects the cut scores to students' locations on the knowledge scale rather than simply to the number of questions they answered correctly.

No matter what procedure is used, cut scores for a test are derived from the collective judgments of people. The experts in the examples described here brought their professional judgments to the task of defining the construct called "knowledge of eighth-grade mathematics" and to the question of how someone who is Proficient on this construct would perform on a particular set of test items. Because of the many subjective judgments made along the way, the cut scores set by the deliberations of these (or any) experts will be estimates only.

Appendix G: Errors in Schools' Mean Scores

In our example, scores on Test A have a standard error of measurement of 30 points ($\sigma_e = 30$), and each of the schools has 400 students ($n = 400$). Then the mean (average) scaled score for the school will have error as well, and the standard error of the mean score for each school, $\sigma_{\bar{x}}$, can be found in this way:

$$\sigma_{\bar{x}} = \frac{\sigma_e}{\sqrt{n}} = \frac{30}{\sqrt{400}} = 1.5$$

So, we can be 95 percent sure that the school's actual mean score falls within ± 3 points (two standard errors) of the computed value.

One way to compare two schools is to compute the difference between their mean scores. This difference will have error as well. The standard error of the difference between mean scores, $\sigma_{\bar{x}_1 - \bar{x}_2}$, would be as follows:

$$\sigma_{\bar{x}_1 - \bar{x}_2} = \sqrt{\left(\sigma_{\bar{x}_1}\right)^2 + \left(\sigma_{\bar{x}_2}\right)^2} = \sqrt{1.5^2 + 1.5^2} \approx 2.1$$

Two schools would have to have mean scores that differed by more than 4 points (two standard errors) to be different in the statistical sense.

Index of Terms